Time Like Coins

Colleen Moyne

Time Like Coins

Time Like Coins
ISBN 978 1 76041 669 0
Copyright © text Colleen Moyne 2019

First published 2019 by
GINNINDERRA PRESS
PO Box 3461 Port Adelaide 5015
www.ginninderrapress.com.au

Contents

Home	7
This Old House	8
Feather	11
Four Seasons of You	13
Goldfish	14
Kerbside Dance	15
Landscape	17
Love Simplified	19
Morning Ritual	22
Mother Nature	23
My Mother	24
My Tree	25
New Beginnings	27
New Ride	28
Nightmares	29
Night-time Rendezvous	30
Our Gift	32
Pearls	33
Photographs	35
Play	37
Postcard	38
Proof of Life	39
Reality	41
Scenic Hotel	42
Regal Journey	44
Seasonal Acrostics	45
Seen at Lake Albert	47
Seventy-five Words	48
Silent Stranger	49
Silk Flowers	51

Slide	52
Smouldering Embers	53
Snake	54
Still Believe in Love	55
That's What I Miss	56
The Circle	57
The Fisherman	59
The Man For Me	61
The Other Grandmother	62
This Country Life	64
This Face	65
This One Moment	66
Time like Coins	67
Three a.m.…	68
To My Precious Child	70
Today	71
Future Musings	72
Waiting on Platform Five	73
Wedding Day	74
Vera	75
Winter in the City	77
Winter Morning in the Garden	78
A Wave of Words	80
Winter Night	82
Forest Friends	83
Daily Debate	84
Goodbye is Like a Closing Door	85
In the Soothing Sea	87
Haikus	88
Musical Feng Shui	89
The Show	90
Waiting	92

Home

My day's work is done.
I leave the cold discomfort of suburbia
and point my car toward the welcoming hills.

Traffic subsides
and the skyline opens above me
as the landscape lays out a welcome mat

I'm heading home,
creating distance between the grey and green,
pretending it's for the last time.

I feel enveloped,
drawn, like a mother draws a sleepy child
into the fold of her comforting arms.

Tonight I will savour
the silence of my retreat,
till the dawn calls me back again.

This Old House

My house believes
it's still 1983
and although she wears the era well,
it's easy to tell
she is growing more stubborn with age

In no hurry to change,
she rests comfortably
in her pine-bark and gravel bed,
like a Buddhist sage

Resplendent in cream-coloured fibro
complimented by a red tin roof
that has weathered more
than a few storms
since her youth

Her modest front room
boasts green ivy walls
that sprout from earth-coloured floors
and wind their way upward
around windows and doors
to a once-white ceiling

The kitchen – her heart
shines warm
with Laminex in lime green
perfectly preserved
under layers of Mr Sheen

Her varnished chipboard
doors and drawers
edged with mismatched tile
echo days when cost
was more important than style

In her bathroom she sports
a fetching striped curtain
with a touch of faux chrome
to add a little bling
but here's the thing…

Despite her questionable style
she is a proud old girl
happy to share
glimpses of her past;
snippets of the lives lived there
in those cosy rooms.

Now, she welcomes me
and somewhat reluctantly
allows me – small step by small step
to introduce her
to the modern world.

A coat of paint here,
a new curtain there
but still she resists to a degree
Still she keeps one foot
firmly planted in 1983
uncomfortable with the new
hesitant to take that final leap
into the present day

But I love her this way
a sweet, old-fashioned girl
who wraps me in her arms
like a loving mother
and tells me bedtime stories
of her glory days.

Feather

Time is ignored
and all other thoughts dismissed
as I watch you
from the sidelines of the shore.
I'm drawn by your elegance,
by your elusiveness,
and by the intrigue
of distance between us.
You open your wings
and lift silently
from the water's surface,
banking away into the sun
and I wonder…
if I will ever be closer than this.
If I could,
I would go with you
and fly alongside you
to show you
that you have
nothing to fear from me.
But I remain grounded,
lingering here
on the water's edge,
long after you have dissolved
into the horizon,
watching the ripples
from your departure
slowly make their way
towards the shore.

And then – I see it…
a glimpse of white,
bobbing
on the water's surface;
a discarded souvenir
of this long-distance encounter,
making its way
ever closer to my feet.
I study the delicate lines,
the simple but complex beauty,
the perfect symmetry
of this fragment of you.
This may be the closest I will get,
but it will do for now
and, tucking it into my pocket
like a treasured postcard
– I head home.

Four Seasons of You

Autumn surrounds you
With its rich golden glow
It kisses you with gentle breezes
And turns your eyes to fire.

In winter's chill air
Your cheeks ripen to apple red
Your voice becomes visible
Each word a misty vapour from your lips

Spring highlights your eyes
Spotlit by the sun as it rises.
It lightens your step
and polishes your amber hair.

But summer flatters you most,
when you turn caramel brown
and sweat glistens
like tiny gems on your skin.

When your feet shuffle
out of the constraints of shoes
and revel in the feel
of sand between your toes.

Goldfish

Small goldfish
swim back and forth
in a pet shop aquarium,
like models on a catwalk
parading their colours.

Silken tails
wave seductively
in the clear water
as they glide and turn
among green foliage.

One ventures close
catching my eye.
Her translucent fins
tread water
as she pauses for effect.

She is lovely,
but one of many
swimming here in circles –
as goldfish do –
for the enjoyment of others.

I watch for a moment
then turn and leave,
heading back to work,
to my own goldfish bowl
on the fifteenth floor.

Kerbside Dance

She shuffles unsteadily toward me.
The rhythmic tap
of her cherrywood cane
echoes on the concrete path.

Grey shawl draped
like a shroud around her bent frame,
the once downy pile
now threadbare and limp.

I see her struggle,
one fragile hand
grasping the cane,
the other a patchwork bag.

Pausing at the kerb
she turns,
eyes me cautiously,
her expression a question mark.

Without words
she communicates
her trepidation at the wide expanse
of bitumen before her

Cars speed past,
no time or patience
for a slow old woman.
Smiling, I offer her my arm.

She takes it gracefully,
her touch feather-light
and together we step into the street
like dancers taking the floor.

Landscape

Inspired by a Dulux colour chart…

A kaleidoscope of colours
fans out before me
like the tail of a posturing peacock.
Every colour of the country
displayed on a palette of paper squares.

Shades of the sea
in Silver Illusion, and Aqua Delight,
and from the beaches:
Sun-bleached Bone,
Corn Silk and Gold Rush.

An array of greens
reflects the lush forest:
Soft Sage and Emerald Mist,
the muted greys of Windspray
 and Rocky River Bank.

Golden Wash portrays
a dry field in summer,
rich rustic deserts glow
in Burnt Ginger,
Bronze and Copper.

Wild flower colours
of Scarlet Ribbon,
Mulberry Passion and Jamaican Gold,
vivid and flamboyant
as a rainbow lorikeet.

They are all there in the swatches –
the colours of Australia;
The colours of a country
rich with life and landscape,
available for purchase
in a four-litre can.

Love Simplified

Love isn't always
hearts and roses
moonlight and violins,
or gifts on Valentine's day.
Love ---real love –
is defined
by tiny moments
that flicker and blink
and take up
mere nanoseconds
in the grander scheme
of life.
Love is the little stuff –
like letting her have
the last slice
of pizza,
or picking up blue cheese
at the supermarket
because you know
it's his favourite,
or hanging the washing
because you know
she's had a busy day.
Texting that funny meme
because you know
it will make him smile,
or bringing her flowers
just because…
because you don't need a reason
to bring her flowers.

Love is taking turns
with the remote
or having a conversation
instead of watching TV.
It's that secret wink
or raised eyebrow
that speaks a hundred words.
A silent
nanosecond gesture
that booms
and reverberates.
Love doesn't always
need to be reminded
or reassured or tested
or proven in expensive ways.
It needs few words
but those words
are warm and soft
and chosen with care.
Time-tested love
knows when
to rush in
and when to retreat,
when to touch
and when to leave be,
when to stay…
and when to go.

If he is there
when you need him,
if she listens
when you pour out your heart.
If her presence
is a warm blanket
or his smile is familiar
as the sunrise.
That's love.
That's all.
That's enough.

Morning Ritual

Alarm sounds, drawing me up
out of my dream-filled sleep.
Reaching out, yawning and slow
to silence the deafening beep.

Slippers on, robe in a twist,
shuffling out of my room.
Sun peeps through slatted blinds,
lighting the morning gloom.

Coffee pot in the kitchen waits,
kettle is on to heat.
Aroma wafts, clearing my head,
warming me to my feet.

Coffeed up and cosy now,
resolve beginning to crack.
Work can wait, no need to rush
and my bed is calling me back.

Slippers off, curtains closed,
robe tossed in a heap
snuggled up beneath the quilt
I drift off back to sleep.

Mother Nature

Mother Nature is dressed
for a fashion show,
styled to impress,
with a golden glow.

Freshly showered
with the dew of dawn,
wearing a gown
of lush green lawn

Donning a perfume
of fragrant flowers,
she parades herself
in the daylight hours

To the birds happy song
she dances and swoons
and at night falls asleep
in the arms of the moon.

My Mother

My mother lived most of her days
on a green floral couch,
thin body folded up like an old linen sheet,
legs tucked beneath her pale frame.
Milky eyes…squinting
through smudged glasses
at a fifteen-inch screen.
Weekday talk shows
and weekend footy…
following the movement
though not really understanding the game.
This is where she sat
from breakfast to bedtime,
so intent on the lives played out
on the flickering screen
that her own life tiptoed away
without her knowing how or when.
On Thursdays
I would ring the doorbell…
she would come
creaking and shuffling,
her bent fingers fumbling with the lock
and seeing me there
would smile feebly…and shuffle back
to fold herself up
on the couch again.

My Tree

There is a tree
down by the water's edge
that calls to me
when I'm there.

It invites me to share
its shady embrace,

and though
there are others
in this quiet place

this tree
is one of a kind.

I consider it mine

We share things –
this tree and I –

like best friends
meeting for coffee
but without the need
for conversation –

just quiet
contemplation.

This tree holds stories
within in its arms,
within the folds
of its skin,
within each knot
and scar.

And so do I.

We are

two of a kind

and that's why

I consider it mine.

New Beginnings

It takes courage
to start again,
to cease life somewhere
and begin it again
somewhere else…

It takes daring
to pack your bags,
to walk away from the known
and venture forth
into the unknown…

It takes resolve
to turn the page
to erase the harsh words
and start to write
a new story.

It takes a friend
to have your back,
to understand that it had to end,
and to be there
when you begin again.

New Ride

Sleek, red machine weaves into view
Sun glinting on mirrored chrome
Vision of vanity
Pictogram of pride
This elegant new ride
testament to a life of toil…

Trophy earned for staying the distance

Erudite elder behind the wheel
Sun glinting on silver hair
Working life done
New ride begun
Cheerfully reclaiming
a youth once lost…

Accelerates into the distance

Nightmares

On a chilly April night,
rough winds drag
the branch of a gum tree
across my window.

Uneasiness mounts
with each creak and moan.
Fear now blooms into panic
as shadows play tricks.

Perhaps it's not the wind I hear
but something more?
I suspect the monsters
of my nightmares

are tampering with my window locks
…and my mind.

Night-time Rendezvous

Winter sky
fades to black,
streets begin to empty
as weary workers wind their way home.

Stars flicker into life
like distant torches
lighting the way
for adventurous night-time creatures.

Tardy birds
hurriedly return to nests
and fluff their feathers
against the approaching chill

smoke wafting from wood fires
mingles with kitchen scents
as families settle down
to dinner and prime-time television.

But while others
close their curtains
against the cold and retreat
to the warm cocoon of their beds

I wrap myself
in coat and scarf,
pull on warm boots
and step out into the blackness.

This is my time
Time to rendezvous with the night
and let its cool, comforting hand guide me
through the sleepy streets.

This is our secret
the night and I
we walk together in silence
like lovers long past the need for words.

Careful not to take
this time for granted
but to savour the sweet, dark silence
in each other's company
till dawn hurries us home.

Our Gift

I've seen those eyes before –
gentle doe eyes, with auburn lashes,
that regard me with young curiosity.

That smile has been smiled before –
I've seen it beam a hundred times
at the simplest of pleasures.

That chin has been here before –
it graced the face of those that precede her,
that led the way for her coming.

That precious heart has lived before –
in her mother, her aunts and in me
it is our gift to her – our legacy.

Pearls

(Cordonostic poem)

Silver hair
curls on furrowed brow
reflecting shafts of sunlight.

Hands, soft as old leather gloves,
curl upon her lap
in repose.

Tiny lines
etched on velvet skin
impart tales of life well lived.

This woman, blessed with vision
bestowed by the years,
sits in grace.

Looks within,
draws on memories
of times long before today.

I watch and wait in silence
as cautiously she
weighs her words,

chooses well
the pearls of wisdom
that she will bequeath to me.

Pearls born of hard times endured,
experience gained,
wounds survived,

knowing that
someday, years from now,
those pearls will be mine to give,

to share with those who follow
while I, silver-haired,
sit in grace.

Photographs

Do you remember when…? you ask
as you pour tea into floral cups.
Ah, yes, I say,
conjuring a picture in my mind
of that faux-happy time.

I see us as children,
riding the red three-wheeler bike
or splashing in the
inflatable swimming pool
edged with blue cartoon whales

I see these vividly,
but only as
glossy squares, edged in white.
preserved in plastic sleeves
between gold-embossed covers.

These are not the real memories;
I renounced them long ago.
These are objects
presented as evidence
of childhood fun,

clues without confirmation,
images with no back-up information.
filed away under 'F'
for false representation.
The real memories were laid to rest

Long ago, beneath layers of life
and now all I share
are glossy squares in plastic sleeves.
If there were no photographs,
there would be no memories.

Play

Big sister, little brother
play happily on the floor.
Blocks become a building,
a book becomes a door.

Young imaginations
flicker and ignite
as pegs and spoons and kitchen tongs
take on another life.

A humble yellow shoebox
becomes so much instead;
first a rumbling school bus
then a teddy bear's bed.

TV goes unwatched,
DVDs unseen,
game consoles ignored,
blank computer screens.

No time for those –
There are cities to evolve,
plans to be made,
problems to be solved.

This is learning,
a time of discovery,
of crafting and creating –
play as it is meant to be.

Postcard

You sent me a postcard today…

A photograph
taken beside a calm sea,
dusk falling, silhouettes backlit
by sun spilling into water.

A six-by-four-inch slice of heaven.

Lovers
embrace on golden sand,
tender smiles, perfectly posed,
perfectly timed, picturesque.

I turned the postcard over.

Your words,
scribbled hastily over latte
in a busy sidewalk café
summarise your delight.

'Having a wonderful time!'

… Wish you were here…

Proof of Life

The river is my happy place.
I go there each day
for quietude and peace

Its ever-flowing,
life-giving energy
recharges my spirit.

But today I have come
seeking solace,
seeking proof of life.

Today I lost
a treasured friend,
a sudden ending to something
that seemed
so tangible and solid.

A jolting reminder
that sometimes
the thread that holds us here
is thin – and prone to breaking.

So today,
I need to be reminded

that, even though
there are endings,
there are also joyous, new beginnings.

And here it is –
Here I find proof of life
on a day when I need it most.

A little mother duck
with four precious babies
cuddled close.

She is aware of my presence
but lets me watch
as though knowing
that this is what I need today.

I am entranced
by these tiny, precious beings.
They, too, are fragile

but so full of life
as they squabble
and ruffle
and toss like paper boats
on the water's surface.

I see the Mother
encircle them
with love and protection.

Today I needed this;
I needed to see again
the beginning of the cycle

I needed proof of life,
and proof of enduring love.

Reality

Underneath my bed, in an old suitcase,
neatly folded with reverence and care,
dwell the garments of my other self –
the fitter, slimmer, confident self.

These garments are a mocking reminder
of 'Pie in the Sky' dreams,
of 'Maybe Someday' plans,
of next summer's goals.

Now and then they see the light of day,
carefully lifted out and measured up,
seeming smaller with each passing year –
and further out of reach.

But the reality self, the mirror self
knows these garments will remain
unworn, unseen, undisplayed
A neatly folded testament to inevitable middle-age spread.

Scenic Hotel

The Scenic Hotel,
once the stomping ground
of my care-free, hope-filled youth;
fond memories
draw me back to this place
and my heart skips
as my eyes rove
over the familiar red brick
and high-pitched roof.

Though years have passed
and life has flown,
the Scenic Hotel remains,
but I dare not enter,
I dare not chance to see
the changes that may lie within,
I dare not spoil
the memories so vivid
that I carry in my heart.

For a moment
I am young again,
wrapped in thoughts
of smiling young men
hovering at the bar,
swallowing Dutch courage
shuffling awkwardly
and planning
their opening lines.

I recall one memory
above all others
of a lanky young man;
a shy one,
with deep brown eyes
and unkempt hair
who held me tight
and spoke
promises of love.

But now I am drawn
back to the present
as a strong hand clutches mine.
I look into
those familiar brown eyes,
reach up and stroke
the hair, still unkempt
but now pepper-grey
and together we turn and walk away.

Regal Journey

The early morning drive begins,
the road ahead is empty.
No other cars dare
to share this space.

A symphony on CD
heralds my passage
and birds hover overhead
ensuring my safe journey.

This autumn day parade of one
consisting of only me
glides regally by
while nature looks on.

Rows of trees
in their very best colours
line the roadside
to honour my presence.

Fields of grass bow and wave
in respect as I pass by.
The hills are turned out
in their tailored green gowns.

Wise old gums
form a guard of honour,
a tunnel of dappled sunlight
to guide me on my way.

Seasonal Acrostics

Autumn

Amber leaves parachute from trees
Ushering in the cooler, frostier days.
Tiny creatures prepare for winter's coming.
Under the earth, green seeds awaken
Making their way up toward the gentle sun –
Nature at its busiest.

Winter

Winter creeps quietly upon us
Ice crystals decorate gardens and car windows
Night air fills with the scent of wood fires
Taking me back to life in the green hills
Each morning breath a white vapour in the cold air
Reminiscent of warm coffees clutched in gloved hands

Spring

Sunny days, bright with anticipation
Playgrounds come once more to life
Ringing with the laughter of excited children
Ice cream vendors ready their trucks to begin rounds
New growth springs from
Gardens green with young growth.

Summer

Sunburnt hills languish
Under the relentless sun
Making tinder for hungry bushfires.
Man and beast retreat into shade
Eager for the seasons end, and
Ready for the relief of cooler days.

Seen at Lake Albert

A flame-coloured sun
hovers patiently on the horizon
illuminating distant hills with a soft halo glow.

Above the hum of insects,
circling lazily in the dry heat
I hear the quick, heartbeat thrum of a lone bird's wing
as it lifts itself languidly from the earth.

A miniature tornado
of fine ochre dust
forms in its wake, swirling and chasing.

And emerging from this jumble of colour
a tiny, blue kingfisher ascends to the sky
shaking the dust from its velvet feathers
as it flies toward the sunsets embrace.

Seventy-five Words

(In seventy-five words)

She held the note
in trembling hands;
so few words

Seventy-five in all;
the final paragraph
in their life story

Twenty years of laughter,
joy, sadness and tears,
memories and milestones

From the first shy meeting,
blossoming romance,
white wedding,

Two children now grown,
a lifetime shared,
so many chapters written

But now she held
in her hands
his goodbye note;

The last paragraph
in the last chapter
of the story of their life.

Silent Stranger

Sometimes they would see her
shuffling silently down the street,
bundled up in an old, grey coat.

No one knew her name,
no one ever wondered,
no one ever spoke.

They kept their distance
from the tattered old recluse
and her tumbledown house.

But with her passing
her silent world erupted.
Along came brothers, nephews and cousins,

A descending, ravenous swarm,
babbling and buzzing,
fracturing the silence, disturbing the dust.

Neighbours watched in awe
as delicate Tiffany lamps
and polished bentwood chairs emerged into sunlight.

Well-kept secrets no longer locked away,
dragged into the street,
loaded onto trucks, piled carelessly into vans.

Sumptuous treasure rooms stripped bare,
fragile mementos snatched up
by greedy fingers and tossed into boxes.

Then, satisfied with their plunder
the swarm buzzed back to oblivion
letting the silence and the dust settle once again.

Neighbours shook their heads
and returned to their bright, busy homes,
the strange spectacle already forgotten.

But tumbling unnoticed along the pavement
a discarded yellow newspaper
held a secret story within its pages;

The tale of a wealthy socialite
broken by loss and heartache;
fugitive from fame, faded into obscurity.

This incurious neighbourhood
unknowing and indifferent,
saw only the façade of an old recluse,

a tumbledown house, a small quiet life,
a silent stranger
bundled up in an old, grey coat.

Silk Flowers

Why do the bereft leave
silk flowers on graves?
Is it to emulate eternal life?
To prove a point
that only real things die,
while skilfully crafted, artificial things
can live forever?
And tell me why some
leave fresh flowers instead?
Do we need another reminder
of the fragility of life,
of the brevity of time?
Are we meant to watch
yet another beautiful thing die?
That is why
I leave you no flowers,
no roses to wither,
no silk substitutes to mock you.
Instead I leave
my private thoughts, my quiet words,
my tears, my memories, my love.

Slide

Warm summer's day, children at play
in the playground down my street
Bright plastic swings and climbing things
and ladders for little feet

I watch my son as he climbs upon
a chunky plastic slide
Above the ground he gazes down
and away he begins to glide

As I watch him play I remember a day
a long, long time ago
When I was eight and couldn't wait
to slide to the ground below

But once at the top I couldn't stop
the fear from taking hold
It's a tempting sight but a fearsome height
when you're only eight years old

Smouldering Embers

Distant rooster calls
paying homage to the sun.
Limber saplings practise
their morning bends and stretches.
Wildflowers shiver awake,
shaking off the last drops of night,
while early birds catch proverbial worms
to share with their eager young.
Sipping the day's first coffee
I begin to dissolve
into shades of blue and gold
mingling with the sky
and sun-bleached hills.
This is all I need right now –
a coffee, a canvas chair,
the smouldering embers
of last night's campfire.
A moment to visit the world
where I was meant to live,
a moment to feel my soul
slide into its proper place.
Tomorrow I will lose
my canvas chair to a cubicle
and my campfire to a computer
but I will never lose
the smouldering embers of today.

Snake

I barely glimpse its movement,
a blip on the radar
as I scan the yellowing grass
mentally calculating
how long I can delay the next mow

But it's there, all right
visible only by a faint tremor
and a flash of glossy brown skin

I want to approach,
to get a closer look,
fear and fascination in conflict.

But fear wins out, and I know
that this beautiful thing and I
cannot share this place.
One of us does not belong
and it should be – but can't be – me.

Still Believe in Love

I haven't had the best of runs
when it comes
to matters of the heart,
when it comes
to finding that 'special someone'
but I still believe in love.

Despite my best intentions,
my judgement has been
somewhat blind,
when it comes
to choosing traits
that complement mine
but I still believe in love.

And even though I've chosen
to walk through life alone,
secure on my path,
happy with my singularity,
content in the quiet company
of pets and books,

I still feel a melting warmth
when I see two lovers kiss.
When the underdog wins the girl
in the made-for-TV movie,
they restore my faith in love.

I'm glad to see the world still turns,
to see my children grow and venture forth,
to find their own 'special someone,'
glad to see the circle complete,
glad I still believe in love.

That's What I Miss

I miss it, you know…
I miss the smell of you.
Hard-work sweat, cigarettes, aftershave,
the birthday roses that you gave.
That's what I miss.

I miss the sound of you.
Guitar strum, baritone hum, gentle words,
the sweet songs now unheard.
That's what I miss.

But most of all
I miss the feel of you.
Stubbled face, loving gaze, open arms,
the blanket of your body as it warms.

That's what I miss

The Circle

I hover helplessly
watching you tremble
as waves of pain wash over you,
consuming, crippling your fragile will.

You are my child;
I want to make it stop,
kiss it better, yet I know my place,
my role in this unfolding scene.

As your pleading cries
echo through the room
a strong, loving hand
reaches down, locks into yours.

Not my hand
but a hand that I entrust
to hold you firm as I have done
and guide you through this rite of passage.

His steady voice,
as familiar to you now as mine,
wraps itself around your fear
with whispered words of faith and pride.

And then –
amidst this loving scene,
a brand-new life emerges,
slipping triumphantly into this world.

We see through tears,
through a frantic flurry
of hands and plastic tubes,
this tiny girl that completes a family.

Fear and pain give way
to sleepy, sweet contentment.
Cooing and rocking this precious child,
I know now that the circle is complete.

There is still a place for me.
My heart swells with joy and trepidation
as I see my daughter become a mother
and I become a proud grandmother.

The Fisherman

Baited rod in hand
and the customary blue esky
by his side,
he sits, lost in contemplation
of the surrounding expanse
of blue-grey river.

Now and then
the quiet surface ripples
with movement from below
while pelicans and gulls glide overhead
observing, vying for the chance
to do a little fishing themselves.

This peaceful tableau repeats
at evenly spread intervals
along the river's edge,
each man mindful
not to encroach on another
or to risk obligatory conversation.

They come here
not to interact with others,
nor to participate
in fun-filled, frolicking adventure.
Their mission is clear,
their reason for venturing here

is to leave behind
the nine-to-five
to seek solace and silence
beside the rippling river
with only birds for company
and the occasional tasty whiting for tea.

The Man For Me

You can keep the man with the six-pack abs,
he isn't really my cup of tea.
I like the man with the crooked smile
and the laughing eyes, who sings off-key.

You can have the one in the tailored suit,
he doesn't do a thing for me.
Give me the man in the baggy blue jeans
bouncing a baby on his knee.

A man who drives a prestige car
is not a high priority.
I want the one who takes the time
to write romantic poetry.

I don't care for a wealthy man,
he's not the one I want to see,
but the man who likes the simple life,
now, he's the kind of man for me.

The Other Grandmother

I liked her – the other grandmother
she had a broad smile
and a broad embrace
for everyone she met.

She was a little ditzy
but surprisingly wise
and devout
and I remember
how she tottered about

on heels a bit too high
for her ample frame
but just the same
she had an air of glamour
and a taste for bling
with sequins and things
and a ring
on almost every finger.

I liked her.
Our grandchildren loved her
and she went too soon.

To her
I was the other grandmother
and she liked me too.

We were a contradictory pair
she, a woman of colour and flair
and I, a little more subdued –
both matriarchs of a growing brood.

We were
happy to share
the children's affection,
were not precious about
who was the flavour of the day
or who got more cuddles than whom.

There was plenty of room
in their hearts for both of us.
Plenty of love, plenty of laughter
and we thought –
plenty of time.
But she went too soon.

And now they must learn
the truth about life
and it's inevitable end
In time, their hearts will mend.

And me?
No longer one of a pair
I'm sad that she is no longer there
Sad – yet aware
of the legacy she entrusted to me.
No longer the other grandmother.
No longer is there a 'we'.
Now there is only me.

This Country Life

Winter sky darkens,
the day melts around me,
yellow sun dissolves into the horizon.

Cooing gently,
white doves settle into nests,
full-bellied chickens march back to their coop.

Chores complete,
I brush away garden dust,
kick off mud-encrusted shoes.

Safe inside,
fireplace stirs into life,
curtains close ranks against the night.

Embraced in warmth,
yielding to weariness,
dinner bubbles to a Brahms waltz.

Wrapped in the arms
of this simple country life
I descend into peaceful serenity.

This Face

I study the face in the mirror;
not with thoughts of vanity or pride
– only curiosity.

This is not a pretty face
but a well-worn face with etched grooves
where frowns and smiles fit.

A face that introduces me
to new friends, strangers and sociable dogs,
with a crinkled smile.

A source of fascination
for the grasping hands of babies
and for children new to timeworn skin.

Each reunion with old friends
an updating of memories, to include
the newer, older me.

I love this wrinkled face,
a face that has seen the slow transition
from youth to maturity.

This face that reflects
a life well-lived, a soul well-grown, a heart well-filled.
The face of happy old age.

This One Moment

I hold this new child
in arms that now seem
too large,
hands that seem clumsy

I raise him to my cheek
to feel the velvet skin
and tiny beating heart

In this one moment,
I see a whole lifetime
I see growing pains

First-day-of-school nerves
first love, and first
crushing heartbreak

I see him venturing
on roads well-travelled,
by those before him

but taking new turns
and finding new paths

This child
My gift to the world
My 'pay it forward'
My thank you
My recompense
For my own precious life.

Time like Coins

One year ago we sat, two young people in love
with only each other in our eyes

Our hearts driven by the stir of adventure,
the rapturous lure of exploration.

On that day we dreamed, pen in hand,
charting our future on a map.

Year one would be Paris, year two perhaps Rome?
With only each other in our lives.

On that day we planned time like coins
to be spent on wishes and whims.

But then came stirrings of another life,
foretelling adventure of another kind.

On that day our plans turned a corner –
charted a different course of exploration.

Today we sit, two young people in love
with dreams of our child in our eyes.

Three a.m....

When all of my insecurities
begin to ring like alarm bells,
dragging me awake
from much needed sleep.

I turn over
and pull the covers tight,
squeezing shut my eyes in feigned sleep,
hoping it will silence them.

But they persist,
tapping at me and calling my name,
demanding my attention
despite the late hour.

A sip of water,
a bathroom break, a page or two
yet still they linger,
knowing that they will soon win.

They will taunt
and poke until I concede;
until I allow them
to climb under the covers.

Then together
we will lay in the darkness
re-living every poor decision,
every loss, every hurt.

We will embrace
like lovers after a quarrel,
knowing that we are accustomed
to each other's company.

Thus we will stay
until the slow transition
from dark night to bright dawn
brings the distraction of another day.

To My Precious Child

If I could say one thing to you now
and know that it would steer
the course of your life

it would be this one thing –

Never lose your childish wonder.
Never lose the fascination
for exploring things
that are new to you.

Never lose the thirst to learn
and never, ever
take anything in this world
or in your life for granted.

It is all as wondrous
as you believe it to be
at this moment
and always open for exploration.

This world has a way of jading us
as we grow. Be aware.
Don't let it rob you
of a life of exuberance.

Let the world turn in its way,
let its hardness make you strong,
let its troubles make you kind,

and let its wild beauty
make your childish heart
continue to sing.

Today

Morning dawns
as it has dawned
on many days before.

He rises
and shuffles stiff feet
into old slippers,

straightens aching bones
and squints milky eyes
against the light.

Today
the grandchildren will come
laughing and bouncing,

chattering and stomping,
filling the faded room
with colour.

These days,
so few among the many,
are now the only days he counts.

Future Musings

Where will I be this time next year?
Secure in my place, my space, my niche,
Doing the work I love.

Children no longer at my feet
Free to pursue a future unknown
Spreading my wings at last.

Where will I be in ten years' time?
Slowing my pace, with grace, with style,
Living the life I want.

Now with grandchildren at my feet
Each with a future as yet unknown
Making the circle complete.

And what is my future twenty years on?
Time spent reflecting, collecting, recalling
Memories to keep me warm.

Whiling away the hours and days
Freedom to read, to write and paint
Blossoming in old age.

Waiting on Platform Five

He stands waiting,
waiting on platform five.
'I'll be there,' she promised,
but promises aren't always kept.

His eyes dart
to the old platform clock.
Six twenty-one, six twenty-five,
time shrinking steadily away.

Last call to board,
shrill whistle echoes.
Shoulders slumped in resignation,
he turns toward the train steps.

Then a familiar voice
trickles through the noise
of hissing engine and shuffling feet –
sweet sound of a promise kept.

Wedding Day

She glides down the aisle,
tastefully swathed in white,
a waterfall of lace tumbling in her wake.

All heads turn to watch
this elegant swan approach
creating ripples of sighs all around her.

This is the day
she pledges her future
to the anxious young man at the altar.

This is the day
their lives become immersed
in bills and babies, mortgages and mothers-in-law.

Love wells in his eyes,
a youthful love that blinds him
to the hint of uncertainty welling in hers.

Vera

Powdered colour dragged across delicate skin,
lipstick traced over lips
once plump and sensuous – now dry
and tired of frivolous conversation.

Sparse white eyebrows
hidden under carefully pencilled lines,
one slightly above the other
in a permanent, quizzical expression.

This face is beautiful still –
now with a different kind of beauty.
No longer one of perfect symmetry
or rosy ripeness

but a soft, quaint beauty
with the delicacy of antique lace
or the fragile, ivory-coloured pages
of an old novel.

A face that reflects a dozen lovers,
a hundred hurdles,
a thousand tears,
and a million smiles,

that has watched the world change
and evolve at a pace
impossible for her to match.
Her world these days is simpler.

A tiny room, a comfy chair,
a cup of tea and talkback radio,
carers bustling in and out
arranging flowers and cushions.

Yet every morning begins the same;
Powdered colour dragged across delicate skin,
lipstick traced over dry lips
and that permanent, quizzical expression.

Winter in the City

Umbrellas blossom
at the first sign of rain,
making polka dot patterns
on grey pavements,
bringing much needed colour
to the monochrome day.
I watch from the cosy nook
of my third-floor office,
the darting manoeuvres
of those who missed
the weather forecast
or chose to leave it to chance.
Wet pedestrians hurrying
to the shelter of doorways
and store fronts,
cowering
as though fearful
that the rain means them harm.
Pulling up collars
and turning their backs.
From up here
their pursuits seem futile.
The rain has already
showered them,
rinsed their hair,
washed their coats.
It can do no more.

Winter Morning in the Garden

Stepping outside
into the cool morning,
the frosty air tingles my skin
and rouses my senses.

Steam from my coffee cup
curls around my gloved fingers
warming my bones.

I take a long swallow
exhale coffee-scented vapour
and feel the hot liquid
funnel through my body –

A delicious contradiction
to the coldness
of the sugar-coated landscape.

Fully awake now
I venture forth among the foliage
heavy with frost
and heady with perfume.

Blades of silver grass
crunch underfoot

like shards of translucent toffee
and dewdrops on leaves
reflect a thousand
bright prisms of light
in rainbow colours.

Soon the sun's pale rays
will melt the frost
and this day will become like any other

But for now
this is my secret place,
I am the ice queen
and I rule this crystal kingdom.

A Wave of Words

It's not about what you say
It never is
It's just a wave of words
And nothing more than this

I sense it coming
Always know
Feel the everyday ripple
Build to a burgeoning flow

Not much more
Than a lapping at first
A rocking to and fro
A seemingly harmless banter
Yet laced with innuendo

And then begins the swell
The advance and retreat
And the subtle shifting
Of the sand beneath my feet

And here it comes,
The surging wave
Heaving, rushing
Lost in shades of blue

Unable to save myself
From being carried along,
Dragged along
Engulfed in a wave of words.

Crashing, tumbling
Until I admit defeat
And then…retreat
Back to the silence of the sea
The everyday ripple
Of you and me

It seems absurd
That this should be
All there is
Just a wave of words…
And nothing more than this.

Winter Night

A dark and drizzly night,
wind-blown trash
tumbling in spirals along my road,
I hurry home, coat drawn tightly
around my body.

Head down
I watch as my boots
splash through rippling puddles,
scattering spilt moonlight
into black shadows.

Safe indoors at last
I shake off the dampness
of the night
and slowly sink into
my sanctuary's glowing warmth.

Forest Friends

Climbing the low gate
I shimmy into my rucksack,
tuck my hair under a hood
and head toward the quiet forest.

This is where I come
when I need to clear my head,
order my thoughts
or find inspiration.

Today I seek the company
of the silent pines
and the soft, mossy undergrowth
to share my sadness.

As I enter their world
soft breezes whisper
through high branches,
welcoming me like old friends.

These trees see my need,
feel my pain
and seek to comfort me
with their soothing song.

Daily Debate

The dirty plates are piling,
but the sun is brightly smiling.
The floor's in need of mopping,
but I need window shopping.

The doonas need an airing,
but I am way past caring.
The dirty clothes are sprawling,
but the lovely day is calling.

There's fluff upon the stairs
and dog-hair on the chairs,
the carpet needs shampooing,
but the gentle breeze is wooing

I should be baking muffins –
but I feel like doing nothing.
The housework is awaiting,
but still I am debating.

I know I shouldn't stall or
make excuses any more
But…oh look…it's too late
I'm already out the door.

Goodbye is Like a Closing Door

Doors are meant to close
but what matters most
is which side we are on
when the key is turned.

We can lock ourselves in,
reside with the memory
and shut out the world
on the other side

But time wills us
to lay down our grief
in warm covers
and let it rest there.

Time wills us
to gather up our memories
like precious children
and step through the door.

Your grief will drift
into silent slumber
and the key will be there
when you need it again.

The world outside waits.
They see your memories
carried close to your heart
and celebrate them with you

They give you time
and allow you space
to nurse your memories
as they grow and blossom

And when you need to revisit
your grief – it will be there,
resting in warm covers
behind the door.

In the Soothing Sea

Drifting, weightless in the soothing sea,
cool waves lapping at my upturned chin,
rising, falling in rhythm with my breath.
Warm sun comforts my quiescent bones.

No pain, no sound permeates the peace.
In the stillness, nothing else exists.
I surrender to this sacred place.
Slowly, sweetly, I become renewed.

Soon the toils of life will call me back,
ever present – but until they do,
I float alone carried by the tide,
just me…drifting…in the soothing sea.

Haikus

Soft eyes blink placidly
Warm velvet skin against cheek
Gentle equine friend

Moonlit beach
Gentle waves beckon
Tiny turtles answer

Morning shower
Cleansing rain
On thirsty skin

Musical Feng Shui

(Pronounced foong shway)

Wind chimes dance, teased by the breeze;
Aroma of sandalwood drifts lazily;
Bright goldfish waltz in a circular pond...

Choreography of sight, sound, scent and feel.

Good fortune symbols arranged with care;
Elements of earth, air, fire and water all blend
in a delicate orchestration of the senses...

The perfect balance of Yin and Yang.

Serene stone images of Buddhist deities,
Keep watch over garden bed and portico,
Conducting the rhythm of good Chi...

Silent maestros, basking in adulation.

This perfect home, built on Feng Shui foundations;
With décor composed by ancestral wisdom,
Takes a bow to ancient superstition...

Health, wealth and happiness fine-tuned.

The Show

The curtain rises,
the show begins.
He has an issue he needs to air
and since I am the only one there
I bear the brunt
of his disgruntled rage

He has the stage
and I am the audience of one
a witness to the show
with no choice to leave
no safe place go

Trapped between
this familiar scene
and the next
destined to watch
replay after replay
of the same day
in the same way
Anxious for the show to end
and the curtain to close
but I don't suppose
it will be anytime soon

Never a two-way interaction,
never the satisfaction
of a resolution
to this daily drama

But once he has vented
and relented
and exited stage left
all that is left
is the empty stage

No more rage,
no encore or applause
and that's because
the show never
really
ends.

Waiting

Amongst scattered leaves
a tiny brown lizard
camouflaged, hidden,
hibernating from
icy winds
that whip through
the once dense trees,
now bare –
waiting, like the lizard,
for the return of spring.

www.ingramcontent.com/pod-product-compliance
Lightning Source LLC
Chambersburg PA
CBHW062139100526
44589CB00014B/1628